NEW TECHNOLOGY

gaming technology

Chris Oxlade

A⁺

Smart Apple Media

This book has been published in cooperation with Evans Publishing Group.

Published in the United States by Smart Apple Media, PO Box 3263, Mankato, Minnesota, 56002

Printed by New Era Printing Co. Ltd, China

Library of Congress Cataloging-in-Publication Data

Oxlade, Chris.
  Gaming technology / Chris Oxlade.
     p. cm. -- (New technology)
  Summary: "Describes the technology used for creating and playing video games. Includes information on how different platforms work and the direction video game technology may be going"-- Provided by publisher.
  Includes index.
  ISBN 978-1-59920-531-1 (lib. bdg.)
  1. Computer games--Programming--Juvenile literature. 2. Video games--Technological innovations--Juvenile literature. I. Title.
  QA76.76.C672O945 2010
  794.8'1526--dc22
                                    2010044239

June 2011
CAG 1652

9 8 7 6 5 4 3 2 1

Credits
Series Editor: Paul Humphrey
Editors: Kathryn Walker and Helen Dwyer
Designer: sprout.uk.com
Production: Jenny Mulvanny
Picture researchers: Colleen Ruck
   and Rachel Tisdale

Acknowledgements
Title page and cover Junko Kimura/Getty Images; p.6 Chris Fairclough/Discovery Photo Library; p.7 Alex Segre/Alamy; p.8 Paul Laing/Alamy; p.9 David J. Green-technology/Alamy; p.11 Blizzard Entertainment; p.14 and 15 left © 2010 Advanced Micro Devices, Inc. All rights reserved. ATI, the ATI logo, Radeon and combinations thereof are trademarks of Advanced Micro Devices, Inc.; p.15 right CoverSpot/Alamy; p.16 alxpin/?Istock photo.com; p.17 Christos Georghiou/?Shutterstock; p.19 Creative Technology Ltd.; p.21 and p.22 Junko Kimura/Getty Images; p.23 Kim White/Bloomberg via Getty Images; p.24 Zeemote and Zeemote SSL are trademarks of Zeemote LLC; p.25 Kevork Djansezian/Getty Images; p.26 Robert Galbraith/Reuters/Corbis; p.27 Fabrice Dimnier/Bloomberg via Getty Images; p.27 The Sims 3 © 2010 Electronic Arts Inc. The Sims is a registered trademark of Electronic Arts Inc., in the U.S. and/or other countries. All Rights Reserved. Used with Permission; p.29 Copyright 2002-2010 Sony Computer Entertainment Inc.; p.31 Blizzard Entertainment; p.32 Copyright 2002-2010 Sony Computer Entertainment Inc.; 34 HandCircus; p.35 Michael Buchner/Wire Image/Getty Images; p.36 Deshakalyan Chowdhury/AFP/Getty Images; p.37 Peregrine; p.38 Screenshot from Atomage Engine by Branislac Siles; p.39 3DVision is a TradeMark of NVIDIA; p.40 © 2010 Advanced Micro Devices, Inc. All rights reserved. ATI, the ATI logo, Radeon and combinations thereof are trademarks of Advanced Micro Devices, Inc.; p.42 Jung Yeon-Je/AFP/Getty Images; p.43 Elena Elisseeva/Shutterstock.

contents

introduction

Do you love the thrills and spills of car racing on a Microsoft Xbox? Or enjoy exploring magical worlds on a PC? Or perhaps you play soccer games on a Nintendo DSi? Theses games rely on fantastically complex computer technology hidden inside the machines.

Gaming technology is one of the fastest-moving fields of computer science, with new developments unveiled almost daily that improve players' gaming experiences. Today's technology will be out of date in only a year or two.

And although computer games are made for fun, the computer game industry is a serious business—it makes more money than the movie industry.

Gaming technology You've probably played on game consoles, such as Nintendo's Wii, Microsoft's Xbox 360, and Sony's PlayStation. Personal computers (PCs) are also a popular gaming platform. Basic PCs have limited capability as gaming machines, but PCs built for games boast powerful graphics

The Nintendo Wii console uses motion-sensitive technology in its controllers.

The latest type of game console is the smartphone (this Apple iPhone is an example), powerful enough to display 3D graphics.

and sound cards, and special hand-held controllers for playing games. At a more simple level, the latest smartphone technology allows mobile phones to work as mini gaming platforms. All these amazing games depend on cutting-edge electronic technology.

Game programs Gaming technology includes the games themselves. These are programs that run on the hardware platforms. They are extremely complex in the case of games that take place in realistic 3D worlds, taking thousands of hours to produce. There is a wide range of game genres, including puzzle games, platform games, adventure games, sports simulations, and social games.

WHAT'S NEXT?

So, what are the probable near-future developments in gaming technology?

- More powerful game consoles capable of running more complex games with improved 3D graphics.

- Improvements in programming techniques to make game worlds and their characters more realistic and lifelike.

- New ideas and techniques for game controllers.

- Improved images, sound, and additional information for players, such as touch and force feedback (see page 37).

electronics

The incredible gaming technology described in this book would not be possible without the latest advances in electronic technology. Here's a quick guide to that technology.

Logic circuits The electronic circuits in consoles and computers are known as logic circuits. These circuits use electricity to represent information and to carry out the complex decision making and calculations needed to make computer games work. The circuits are made up of components such as transistors, resistors, and capacitors. Transistors are the most important components. They act as electronic switches. Game platforms contain extremely complex circuits containing thousands or sometimes even millions of transistors. The circuits, known as integrated circuits, are built into the surfaces of wafers of silicon, known as microchips.

MOORE'S LAW

Do you have an old game console or two sitting around your home? Most gamers do because new consoles come out so regularly. Improving manufacturing techniques and new technologies mean that the number of components that can fit on a single microchip doubles approximately every 18 months. This rule of thumb was first noted by Gordon Moore, one of the founders of chip-maker Intel.

Microchips are at the heart of every game console—the chips are protected by a plastic case with metal legs that carry electric signals in and out.

A close-up of a graphics processing chip—these are some of the most complex microchips ever made, each containing millions of microscopic components.

Processors and cores The main microchips in any game platform are the central processing unit (CPU) and the graphics processing unit (GPU). Cutting-edge processors have multiple cores, each of which can do the job of a single processor. The cores share the workload, so the processor can do its tasks faster. This is known as parallel computing. Although many modern computers feature multiple-core processors, the full power of these processors is yet to be realized, as computer programmers are still developing techniques to make full use of them. This means that a dual-core processor is not twice as fast as a single-core one. But in the future, parallel processing will produce awesome processing power.

WHAT'S NEXT?

The transistors and other components on microchips are microscopic. The smallest components are just a few nanometers in width (25.4 million nanometers are in 1 inch). One million transistors can fit in a square millimeter on a chip. It is going to be difficult to shrink components much more before they become unreliable. By 2025, it's possible that components could be a quarter of the size they are now, but after that, a new technology based on nanotechnology will have to be found.

CHAPTER 2
game graphics

"Wow—great graphics!" shouts your friend as you demonstrate the new car-racing game you just bought. Graphics are often the most impressive feature of a computer game. They show the objects in the game world, game information, such as menus, options, scores, weapons, and energy levels, and also video clips. So, how does a machine generate these on-screen pictures for you?

The majority of games feature either two-dimensional (2D) graphics or three-dimensional (3D) graphics. 2D graphics are used for games such as board games and platform games, where objects and characters move over a static or scrolling background.

Graphics basics In your car-racing game, the on-screen image of the cars and landscape is made up of a grid of thousands of colored dots, known as pixels (that's short for picture elements). The image that

MODEL WORLDS

Imagine the world of a racing game. In a computer's memory, the 3D world of the game is made up of objects which make up the cars, the track, the landscape, trees, buildings, spectators, and so on. The surface of each object is made up of flat geometric shapes called polygons, and each polygon is defined by its corners, or vertices. Curved surfaces, such as car bodies, are made up of many small polygons. The polygons are also known as primitives, because they are the basic building blocks of the game world. Each polygon has a color and a texture to make it look realistic.

Dozens of simple polygons joined together make up the complex shape of this dolphin. Each polygon has three corners, or vertices.

appears on screen is a visual copy of data held in the computer's video memory. To display an image, the computer must calculate the color of each and every pixel and store the results in the video memory.

Three-dimensional graphics Car-racing games (and many adventure and combat games) are set in worlds where you can drive or wander around. They are three-dimensional (3D) worlds, and they are shown with 2D graphics. As you move around, the image you see of the world changes. 3D graphics are much more complicated to display than 2D graphics, so they require much greater processing power.

SPRITES

A sprite is a small 2D image that can be placed anywhere on screen, and also scaled (made larger or smaller), rotated, and moved. In 2D games, sprites are used to display objects, such as spacecraft and missiles. In some 3D games, sprites are used to display certain objects, such as trees, because they are quicker to display than 3D objects.

A screenshot of the complex 3D world of the online game World of Warcraft. *Every object, game characters included, is made up of polygons.*

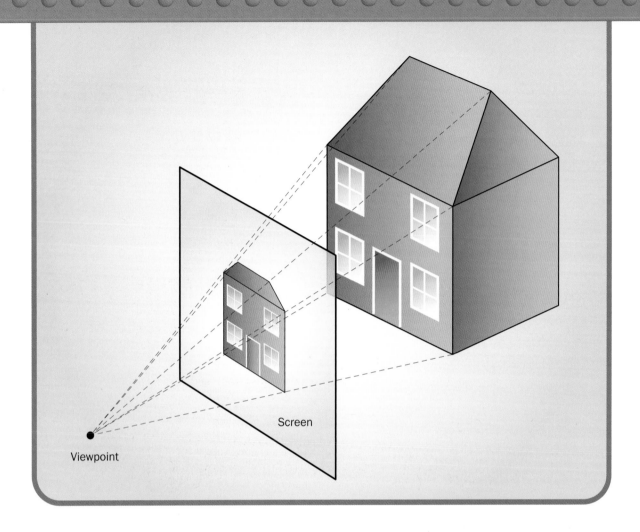

Viewpoint

Screen

The screen is a window through which you see objects in a game world. The computer "maps" the polygons of the objects into shapes on the screen.

Rendering How do we get from a mathematical model of a game world to an image of that world on the screen? The answer is a process called rendering. And it's complicated—very complicated. The computer must calculate what each polygon in the world looks like from a particular viewpoint, which is normally the player's position. It calculates where on the screen each

WHAT'S NEXT?

As computers become more powerful (which means they can process more information more quickly), they can display more complex 3D worlds. That means the worlds that you play games in can have more objects, more detail, and more complex textures. They can also have more realistic lighting effects.

polygon in the world will appear and which ones will be hidden behind others. Then, it draws the polygons with the correct textures and colors, with the right reflections and shadows.

But that's just one frame. To create smooth action as your car rattles along a track or your character runs through a world, the computer needs to carry out this rendering process from scratch 25 or more times per second (see also frame rates on page 16).

Video memory Video memory (or video RAM) is where images that are displayed on screen are stored. The memory holds information about the color and brightness of each pixel in the image. There is normally space for two or more frames to be stored, so that one can be displayed while the next is produced. Textures are also stored in video memory ready to be used in rendering.

The same object in its "wire-frame" form, with polygons filled in and shaded, and with textures added to the polygons.

HOW IT WORKS

Here's what a computer does to render a scene. The process involves millions of mathematical calculations.

- translation: determining the position of polygons in the game world in relation to the viewpoint.
- depth sorting: working out the order of the polygons from near to far because polygons far away can be hidden by polygons that are close by.
- lighting and shadows: adjusting the shade of polygons due to light and shadow, and adding highlights.
- projection: calculating where each polygon will appear on the image that will appear on the screen (i.e. converting the 3D world into a flat image).
- texture mapping: applying color and patterns to the polygons in the image that is in the video memory, ready to be displayed on screen.

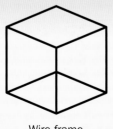

Wire frame

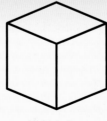

Hidden line

Solid lit

Texture mapped

Graphics processing units

Crunching through all the calculations needed for you to enjoy those high-speed action games is a very special item—the graphics processing unit (GPU). A GPU is a microchip that is dedicated to performing the operations needed to draw 3D graphics (and also some 2D graphics). It can do these operations at lightning speed—faster even than a general central processing unit (CPU). And it also frees up the CPU for other jobs. Some GPUs can be linked together to share work and speed up the rendering process (these technologies include ATI's Crossfire technology and NVIDIA's SLI technology). In the future, more powerful graphics will result from "parallel" processing like this.

A shiny, new GPU doesn't stay at the cutting edge of gaming technology for long. You can bet that a faster, more powerful processor will be along a few months later. Top-end GPU cards for PCs are expensive, often costing more than complete game consoles. They are some of the most complex microchips ever made, with more than 2 billion transistors.

A graphics chip designed to be "embedded" in arcade games machines.

MEASURING SPEED

The speed of a GPU is often measured in polygons per second and texture fill rate. Polygons per second is a measure of how many polygons the GPU can process—cutting-edge GPUs can draw more than 800 million. Texture fill rate is how many pixels can be drawn on screen every second. For modern GPUs, the figure is a staggering 50 billion or more!

Down the pipeline Let's go back to the rendering process. A whole series of calculations is done on the data as an image is rendered. Computer programmers say that the data goes down a "graphics pipeline," which ends

An ATI Radeon GPU card (left) for a PC. The GPU chip is hidden under the fan, which keeps the chip cool as it does its work. On the right are connections for the computer; at the bottom left are connections to the screen.

with the image in video memory. Most of the work in the graphics pipeline is done by a GPU.

In a car-racing game (right), data about the cars, track, and surrounding structures is fed into a graphics pipeline, and data for the on-screen image drops out the other end.

HOW IT WORKS

The main work in the graphics pipeline is done by parts of the GPU called shader units. These are programmed to do different rendering tasks, such as calculating translations (see page 13) and adding textures to polygons. As GPU technology advances, shader units will do their jobs more and more quickly.

Lighting effects add realism to computer-generated images. Here are accurate reflections from different textured surfaces and transparent materials.

Frame rates If you've played fast-action games, you'll know there's nothing more annoying than jerky on-screen movement. This is caused by low frame rates. Each complete image displayed on screen is a frame. Frame rate is the number of frames that are displayed every second. Frame rates must be above about 25 per second to produce smooth, non-jerky movement on screen. Modern GPUs can display the complex 3D worlds of first-person games such as *Call of Duty: Modern Warfare* at 60 to 120 frames per second at high resolutions, giving super-smooth animation.

WHAT'S NEXT?

Take a quick look around you. You see things because of the way light rays bounce off them (or are bent as they go through them). The ways light rays bounce and bend creates complex reflections and shadows. For example, you might see a shadow created by one object reflected in a curved china bowl behind a glass door.

Lighting effects like this can make computer-generated worlds look ultrarealistic, but they are too complex for today's GPUs to create. But a method called ray tracing simulates the flow of light through a world, allowing transparent objects and multiple reflections. However, ray tracing involves millions of complex calculations. Processors will have to become far more powerful before ray tracing can be used in games where scenes must be drawn dozens of times a second to create animation.

DirectX and OpenGL Look at the "system requirements" for action games, and you're likely to see the mysterious terms DirectX and OpenGL. These are special graphic languages that let a computer's central processing unit tell a GPU what to do. DirectX (used on Microsoft devices, such as PCs running Windows and the Xbox 360) and OpenGL are the most common languages. They are constantly upgraded to take advantage of new technologies of the latest GPUs.

This is the sort of realistic image that a computer can create. Producing this sort of detail at high frame rates needs huge computer power.

WHAT'S NEXT?

Photorealism is the ultimate goal of game developers. Photorealistic graphics are so detailed that they look like pictures of the real world. Computers can already produce photorealistic images, but not at the speeds needed for games. This will require extremely high-speed graphics cards with exceptional resolution—technologies that are perhaps five to ten years away.

Future features Graphics processing units are becoming so powerful that they are better at some mathematical tasks than central processing units are. The next generation of GPUs will use their mathematical ability to add extra rendering effects to the graphics they draw, such as complex lighting effects and textures. DirectX 11 already uses a system called DirectCompute to create shadows and transparency (used to make glass objects see-through).

Game sounds You creep slowly through a dark forest. All you hear is the rustle of leaves underfoot and your own breathing . . . until a terrifying scream comes from behind you. Games simply wouldn't be the same experience without sound effects and background music. They add realism to games, working in combination with graphics. Sounds also provide feedback, telling you when

A typical layout of multiple speakers in a surround sound system.

SURROUND SOUND

The latest game consoles and computer graphics cards can output surround sound as well as stereo sound. Many sound cards also feature 3D positional audio, or virtual surround sound, which sends sounds to stereo speakers at slightly different times to create a surround-sound effect. See page 36 for more about stereo and surround sound.

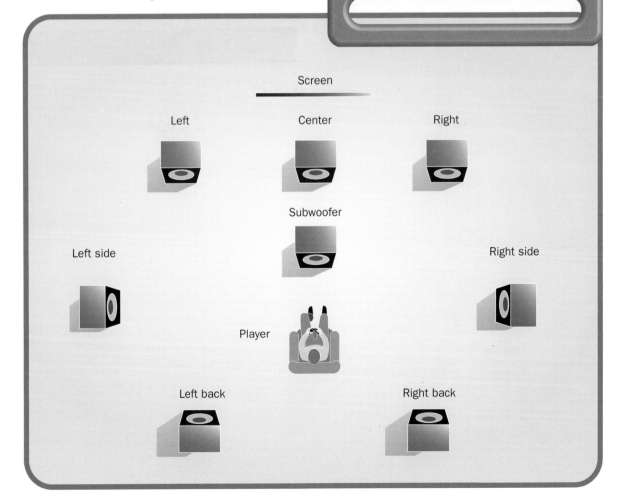

Screen

Left   Center   Right

Subwoofer

Left side   Right side

Player

Left back   Right back

A Creative Sound Blaster X-Fi ExtremeGamerFatal1ty—a PC sound card designed for gaming.

events have happened (for example, when an option has been selected), give you information, and let you communicate in multi-player games.

Stereo and surround sound Stereo sound is used in 3D games so that game sounds appear to come from the right directions. It can also alert players to where other characters are moving around, perhaps unseen.

Computers have special hardware that handles sound. In a PC built for playing games, this is normally a plug-in sound card. A sound card is dedicated to sound, just as a graphics card is dedicated to graphics. It can produce hi-fi quality sound effects, play dozens of different sounds at the same time, and produce surround sound (see page 18). It also takes the workload of producing sounds from the CPU,

WHAT'S NEXT?

Dogs barking, cars crashing, guns firing—game sound effects like these are recorded from the real thing, digitized, and stored in computer memory ready to be played. But scientists are currently producing sounds instead by making computer models of the objects and events that make the sounds. For example, they have produced a dripping sound by modeling how a drop of water landing in a bowl affects the air around it, producing sounds. One day, techniques like this could produce game sounds.

allowing games to run faster (just as a GPU takes workload from the CPU for producing graphics). Graphics cards also have on-board memory where sounds can be stored ready to be played when needed.

There is special software that computers use to control sound cards, such as EAX (environmental audio extensions) and OpenAL (Open Audio Library). Future sound technology will allow for sounds that bounce off objects in game worlds, creating realistic effects, such as echoes and muffled sounds.

CHAPTER 3

game platforms

Which machines have you played games on? The Nintendo Wii? Sony's PlayStations? How about handheld consoles, such as the Nintendo DSi and PlayStation Portable, or personal computers? And what about mobile phones, smartphones (such as Apple's iPhone), and mp3 players? All these machines are gaming platforms.

How consoles work All the game platforms mentioned above can play games, but what's inside each one, and how do they work? What amazing technology can you boast about if you own one of these machines?

The main game consoles (Xbox 360, PS3, and Wii) each have different technical parts and run games and draw graphics in a different way. Each also has a different way of storing games and game data, different player controllers, and different ways of communicating with other devices (including other consoles).

Even though the PS3, Xbox 360, and Wii are a few years old, they are still state-of-the-art consoles. They are known as seventh-generation consoles.

PlayStation 3 At the heart of a PlayStation 3 is a special CPU known as a cell processor. It is typical of the dedicated circuitry in game consoles. The cell contains a PowerPC processor which controls the system. It feeds

WHAT'S NEXT?

If you are a devoted gamer, you're aware of the constant rumors about new game consoles. So, what new machines can you expect to be playing on soon? The next generation of consoles from Microsoft, Sony, and Nintendo (the eighth generation, to replace the Xbox 360, the PS3, and the Wii), is in the pipeline, but there are no details on the new technologies that they might feature. Possible names include the PS4 and Xbox 720. They are likely to be faster versions that are able to generate more complex graphics than the current machines.

computing work to eight other processors known as Synergistic Processing Elements that do the number crunching. The PS3's GPU is a custom-designed chip, called the Nvidia RSX Reality Synthesizer.

Microsoft Xbox 360 The Xbox 360 boasts a PowerPC CPU with three cores. Each core can handle two computing jobs at once. One core might handle sound, one handles graphics, and one moves objects in the game world. It also has a custom-made GPU that features shaders that can work in parallel to speed up the graphics.

Visitors try out new games on Xbox 360 consoles on the Microsoft stand at the Tokyo Game Show in September 2009.

Nintendo Wii The Wii is less powerful on graphics than the PS3 or Xbox. Inside, there is an updated version of Nintendo's older system, the GameCube, with no dedicated graphics processor. The Wii's popularity comes from its control system, which allows players to control games with hand motions—showing that super-powerful graphics are not everything that gamers are looking for. (See page 34 for how the Wii's controllers work.)

Portable gaming The two most popular portable game consoles are the PlayStation Portable (PSP) and the Nintendo DS. Recent versions of the PSP are the PSP 3000 and the PSP Go. The 3000 loads games from DVD-like UMDs (Universal Media Discs) via a small optical drive, but the Go instead follows the trend of having games available only for downloading from the internet. The PSP has a wide screen, an LCD display, two main CPUs, a media processor (that handles video and sound), and a 3D graphics processor that can process 35 million polygons per second. The PSP's network capability allows it to connect with a PS3.

A Sony PSP Go handheld console—one of the first handhelds that downloads games rather than loads them from an optical disc.

A recent version of the Nintendo DS is the DSi XL—an updated DS that features two digital cameras for use in interactive games. It also has larger screens than previous models. Processing power comes from two CPUs.

PC games With the addition of a graphics card with a powerful GPU and a sound card for hi-fi sound, a humble desktop computer is transformed into a serious gaming machine. With the right hardware, a PC can outperform any other game platform for speed, and some graphics cards can drive two or more displays at the same time. There are also more games available for PCs than for other platforms and thousands of free games available online. However, a top-end gaming PC costs several times as much as a game console, and constant upgrades are needed to run the latest 3D games.

Smartphones such as the Palm Pre Plus allow you to take your game playing everywhere you go.

WHAT'S NEXT?

One of the hassles of console game playing is all that plugging and unplugging of wires into the TV. It would be better if the TV were a platform itself. It's possible that in time, TVs will become game platforms. All that's needed is a processor to be built into the TV, and the TV connected to the internet. Then, the TV will download games as you want to play them. The television would have gaming controllers, but you would still have to share the television with other people!

Smartphones The smartphone is the new gaming machine on the block. It's small, but it packs a powerful punch. This really is gaming in the palm of your hand. A smartphone is simply a mobile phone with extra capabilities, such as web-browsing and e-mail. Smartphones normally have larger screens than traditional cell phones and have become popular as portable game consoles. Many games are now written for a system called Google Android, which can be installed on many different smartphones. The processing power of some smartphones, such as Apple's iPhone, allows players to play complex games with 3D graphics.

Game and data storage There's always some waiting around between firing up a console and playing a game. Why? Because the console needs to load the data needed for the game into its memory. And after you've blasted through a game level, data has to be stored somewhere so that you can return for more action another day.

Game consoles normally have an optical drive that loads game software and data from the DVD and Blu-ray discs that games are supplied on. The PlayStation Portable uses its own small optical discs called UMD, and the Wii uses its own type of optical discs that can be read much faster than a DVD. Game saves are stored on a hard drive, internal memory, or plug-in memory cards.

Some game players use their smartphones as platforms so much that they have separate game controllers. This is Zeemote, a wireless Bluetooth smartphone game controller.

HOW IT WORKS

Waiting for smartphones to load online games and data can be a bit of a yawn. It's because most mobile networks, with speeds of around 3 Mbps (megabits per second), are much slower than land-based broadband, with speeds up to 50 Mbps. For now, this makes online gaming on smartphones (and on PCs linked to the internet via mobile networks) impractical. But fourth generation (4G) technology should solve this problem. It boasts speeds up to a staggering 1000 Mbps.

All this fantastic technology may be redundant when the next generation of consoles arrive. The new machines will probably download games exclusively from the internet and store data online (see box on page 31). This is already true of the PSP Go (see page 22).

Communications Those multi-player racing games, sports games, and shoot-em-ups are super fun, but they can only work because game platforms talk to each other. And for that they use internet connections, often through wi-fi. These communications also allow console manufacturers to provide online features, such as Xbox Live and PlayStation Home, where players can interact with others. Connections also allow platforms to download music and video, and browse the internet. A permanent connection to the internet will be a major feature of future consoles.

A demonstration at a gaming conference of Twitter social networking on the online service for the Xbox 360, the Xbox Live community.

FOR AND AGAINST

Consoles connected to the internet.

For
- Players can download new games and updates, and store game data online.
- Players can take part in multi-player online games.
- Allows players to become part of a huge gaming community.
- Allows consoles to become more general entertainment machines, downloading music and data, and allowing web browsing and access to social networks.

Against
- Any loss of internet connection brings gaming to a halt.
- Consoles capable of browsing the internet need parental controls to prevent young children from seeing inappropriate material.
- Children don't know who they are really talking to online or who they are meeting in game worlds.

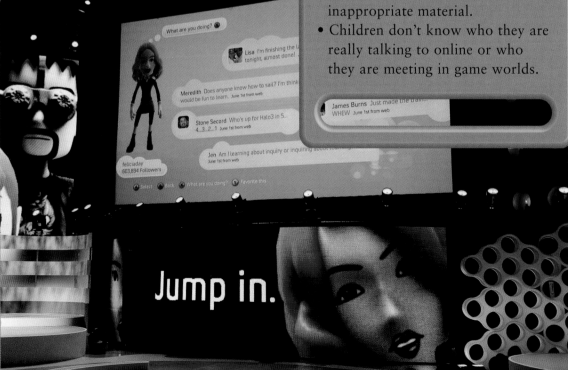

CHAPTER 4
video games

Ever wonder what's actually on those game DVDs and Blu-ray discs that you spend all your money on? Programs and data, that's what. Once loaded, the programs instruct the platform's processor to create the game (i.e. to display the game graphics, control the flow of the game, move objects, and so on). The data is needed by the game, and can be anything from the image of a player's face in a tennis game to the sounds of an explosion, plus video clips and sound tracks.

Game engines Imagine you are playing a football game against your friend. Your player throws the ball towards the goal but it hits the post. How does the console know it hit the post? The answer is smart software that detects collisions between the objects in the game world (in this case, the ball and the goal post).

Collision detection is a tiny part of the program that controls the overall flow of a game, known as the game engine. The engine does the basic game tasks such as loading data that's needed, rendering graphics, moving objects in the game world, detecting collisions, taking input from the player, and so on. Game developers often use ready-made game engines to create particular types of games, adding their own data and rules to make it unique. A well-known example is the Unreal Engine, used to create first-person shooter games.

Playing Splinter Cell: Double Agent. *This game uses the Unreal game engine to control basic tasks.*

A programmer in the process of designing game graphics at the offices of Ubisoft, one of the world's leading computer game developers.

New technology in this area includes game engines for smartphones and for web browsers on PCs.

Game design Some games are five-minute wonders, but others you can't put down. Why the difference? Game design has a lot to do with it. Good game design makes a game playable and absorbing. It's why a cleverly designed game with simple graphics and sound can be more addictive than a poorly designed game with cutting-edge 3D graphics. Increasingly, game developers employ graphic designers, musicians, script writers, and video directors to help develop new games.

PORTING

Most games are available on different gaming platforms, but each platform has its own hardware that is programmed in a different way to achieve the same effect. Developers then must rewrite software to move a game from one platform to another. This is known as porting. Porting to less powerful platforms (e.g. from PlayStation to PSP) requires complex games to be simplified.

WHAT'S NEXT?

Imagine a game world where each leaf and blade of grass sways in the wind, the weather is astoundingly realistic, and the water in streams flows naturally. This super-realistic world is a "Living Breathing World," and it's what game developers are aiming for. In addition, future game worlds will feature true "free-roaming," where players can explore the whole world at will—not just the areas that game play takes place in.

Artificial intelligence Have you ever wondered how that hideous creature follows you, no matter where you hide? Or why it's so hard to beat a computer in a chess game? Artificial intelligence (AI) is the key.

Artificial intelligence is the science of making computers (and other machines) behave in a way that people would. It can make a computer appear to make decisions, solve problems, or learn from experiences like a human would.

In the world of computer games, artificial intelligence techniques are used to make non-player characters (NPCs), such as teammates in a football game or enemy monsters in a role-

WHAT'S NEXT?

Future generations of consoles will probably have some form of built-in artificial intelligence. The consoles will behave like agents (in-game characters) themselves, interacting intelligently with players. As of 2010, this technology is purely software based.

The Sims are simulated people living in a simulated world. Their behavior is controlled by artificial intelligence techniques.

In racing games such as Gran Turismo, *cars controlled by the computer use artificial intelligence to try to block and overtake.*

playing game, behave intelligently. Artificial intelligence is important for adding realism to games, which makes them more fun to play.

Examples of AI in games are pathfinding (see sidebar), computer opponents in a basketball game passing to each other, and cars in a driving game overtaking you or blocking your way.

Artificial intelligence is achieved with software that is part of the game engine. AI technology for games is improving all the time. Increasing computing power allows for more complex software techniques to create more intelligent behavior.

HOW IT WORKS

Let's take a look at an example of AI in a game. One relatively simple application is pathfinding—it's how that monster manages to chase you around. Like all artificial intelligence techniques, pathfinding relies on an agent (the monster) making logical decisions based on data in the game. In pathfinding, the software decides if your character is hidden from the monster, and checks which way the monster is looking. It then calculates a route for the monster to take. As AI improves, agents will become smarter. For example, an enemy might decide to take an elevator instead of the stairs to try to find you!

Future intelligence Where could artificial intelligence take your game-playing experience? Combined with more realistic graphics and interactive game controls, it will lead to better immersion in games (see page 40). Future in-game characters will have emotions and social skills. They will also be able to adapt to the way a player is playing a game, giving different players a different game experience. The ultimate goal of AI for games is that a player can't tell whether an in-game character is controlled by the computer or by another player.

Online games If your game machine is not permanently connected to the internet now, it soon will be. All the software and data for your games will be sold and downloaded from the internet (this is known as digital distribution). Many of today's console and PC games allow multi-player action over the internet, and this trend will continue.

Games on servers One likely development of permanent internet connections will be that the game software will not be on the platforms themselves, but on powerful servers on the internet. The servers will actually run the game engines, doing all the

WHAT'S NEXT?

Imagine playing in a game world that puts computer-generated enemies into the real world! Experts call this augmented reality. It'll be made possible by combining portable consoles and smartphones with GPS and high speed online communications. An example would be a search-and-find game played outside in the streets, with enemies appearing on smartphone screens and player positions tracked by GPS, all controlled by a server on the internet.

object movements and rendering the graphics. The consoles will simply take player inputs and upload them to the server, and also download images created by the game engine on the server (which will be in the form of live video). This system will allow consoles to be much simpler and for complex games to be played on basic computers without the need for even more powerful graphics processors.

Multi-player games Games such as *World of Warcraft* provide a huge world for players to explore, with players represented by characters called avatars. This sort of game is known as a massively multi-player online role-playing game (MMORPG). Each player's console runs a game engine, but data about other players and game characters comes from a central server. As internet speeds increase, these online game worlds are getting more and more realistic. Avatars will soon be capable of natural speech and expressions.

A scene from the super popular online game World of Warcraft. *The different characters here could be controlled by players from opposite sides of the world.*

FOR AND AGAINST

How do online games compare with games on consoles?

For
- There is no need to buy a physical version of a game.
- There are always plenty of opponents to play against.
- Online storage allows for massive, detailed game worlds.
- Games are always up-to-date.

Against
- Online games require a permanent and fast internet connection.
- Platforms are exposed to the dangers of viruses and other malware.
- Players don't know who they are meeting in multi-player games.

CHAPTER 5
game controllers

What's your favorite way of steering a rally car in a driving game or hitting a ball in a tennis game or looking around in a shoot-em-up game? A console controller, a PC joystick, or perhaps a touch screen? Let's have a look at how game controllers work, then move on to some of the amazing technology in the pipeline, which will completely change the way you interact with games.

In computer terms, controllers are inputs to the gaming platform. The game engine uses data from the inputs to decide what happens in the game.

Controller basics Hand-held game controllers contain digital controls (i.e. on and off buttons) and analog controls (i.e. buttons or sticks that control by their position). Wireless controllers send inputs to the console by infrared or radio links, such as Bluetooth. There are also special controllers for particular games, such as steering wheels for driving games, flight sticks for flight simulators, and guitars for rock-band games.

The Sony PSEye forms the base of a motion control system for the Playstation 3. In many games, it's used for gesture control.

WHAT'S NEXT?

In the real world, we communicate with each other by speaking and making facial expressions. Sony is developing a system that allows its PSEye camera to detect faces and facial features, and recognize a player's head movements. In the future, systems with stereo microphones will be able to detect where a player's voice comes from, with the possibility that a console's intelligent agent will turn to face any player who is speaking!

Touch, vision, and hearing Some consoles feature the senses of touch, vision, and hearing, which allow improved interaction with players. Many smartphones have a touch-sensitive screen for controlling games (see below). Vision is provided by cameras. It's used to detect players' body movements, and to put their photographs and videos into games. The Nintendo DSi has twin cameras, and Sony's PSEye is a camera for the PS3. Nintendo's Wii also uses a remote vision sensor bar to track the motion of controllers in the player's hands (more on this on page 32). Hearing is provided by microphones, and allows for voice control of games.

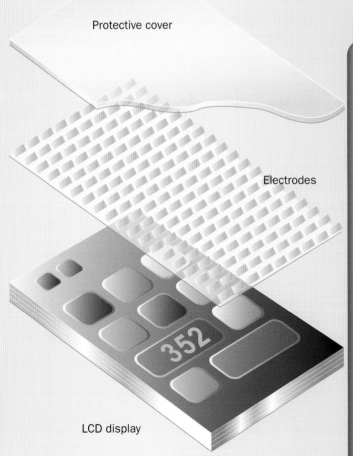

The main layers on the touch screen of a smartphone.

Protective cover

Electrodes

352

LCD display

Electrodes in a smartphone screen sense the touch of a person's finger and transmit an electrical impulse to the processor, giving it information about the location.

HOW IT WORKS

How exactly does a touch screen know where you are touching? There are two popular technologies. A resistive screen (as on the Nintendo DSi) has two layers of material that conduct electricity on top of the screen. A touch makes the layers come in contact, which allows a flow of electricity detected by the device. A capacitive screen (as on the Apple iPhone) has an electrically charged layer on top of the screen. A touch with a finger allows some charge to leak away. The device senses the loss of charge and where it went from.

Motion sensors If you've played any game on a Nintendo Wii, you'll know all about game controllers that detect motion, because the fun of playing on the Wii depends on them. Some handheld controllers and smartphones also contain motion controllers. Motion controls are the future.

The Wii remote controller contains sensors for movement in three directions, and motions around three axes (tipping backwards or forwards, tipping right or left, and twisting). The Wii also keeps track of where in space the controller is by using its sensor bar that detects infrared light coming from the controller. The add-on Wii Motion Plus increases the accuracy of the controller.

Motion sensors inside the Apple iPhone detect the angle of the iPhone relative to the floor, and this

A screenshot from Rolando, *a popular iPhone game. Tilting the iPhone makes the characters roll left or right.*

information is used to control games (such as steering in a driving game).

HOW IT WORKS

How does the Wii's hand-held controller or Apple's iPhone detect your hand movements? The answer is by using tiny specialized microchips. Inside are accelerometers. These detect the motion of tiny weights on springs as the player moves the controller. Similar chips measure the angle of the controller relative to the horizontal plane.

WHAT'S NEXT?

Imagine making your in-game character walk by simply walking in place, or opening a door by simply twisting your hand. Or how about jumping in a sports game and watching your on-screen avatar copy every move? This controller-free technology is available with the Microsoft Xbox Kinect system. A combination of cameras and sophisticated software recognizes the body shape and movement of the player's arms and legs.

A demonstration of Microsoft's Kinect controller-free system for the Xbox. The player is rolling a bowling ball.

Head tracking is a technology that may be used for 3D graphics (page 39 and 40). In this system, the position of a player's head is tracked using positional sensors.

Gesture control The Wii allows the use of natural movements to control games. You can swing the controller like a racket in a tennis game or like a sword in a role-playing game. This is called gesture control, or more technically, a perceptual user interface (PUI). Gesture control will likely be how most games will be controlled in the future. A set of standard gestures may be developed, so that you might use the same gesture to choose from a menu, no matter which console you are playing on.

CHAPTER 6
displays and feedback

Games wouldn't be much fun without pictures and sounds. Read on to discover what amazing technology might soon be making your games more exciting and realistic. Game platforms have outputs that feed information back to you, the player. These include speakers for sound, displays for images, and motion feedback devices.

Speakers The roar of engines, the screech of tires, and the rumble of explosions—sound is an important form of feedback for you as you play a game, so all platforms provide outputs for speakers or headphones. Stereo or surround sound lets you hear that terrible foe or rival race car approaching from one side or the other. The basic surround sound system is 5.1 surround sound, which uses five small speakers and one bass speaker. Better yet, 7.1 surround sound uses 7 small speakers and one bass. The more speakers placed around a player, the more accurately the direction that game sounds come from can be modeled.

Simulator rides tip, tilt, and roll, providing motion feedback for riders (as well as graphics and sound) that convinces them they are flying in a real aircraft.

THEME PARK RIDES

Have you ever been on a motion ride at a museum or theme park? If so, you have experienced motion feedback. Riders sit in seats or inside modules that are moved by hydraulics or pneumatics under control of the ride software. Motion is linked carefully to the images the riders are seeing, fooling them into thinking they are moving. This sort of system may become available for console or PC games one day.

FLIGHT AVIONICS TITAN - 30

WHAT'S NEXT?

An organic light-emitting diode (OLED) is a light-emitting diode that produces light from a layer made up of plastic-like material. OLED displays are extremely thin and use much less power than LCD displays. They are perfect for hand-held consoles and smartphones, and can even be made into flexible screens.

Displays Displays for game platforms are either televisions (in the case of game consoles), computer monitors (in the case of personal computers), or built-in screens (in the case of hand-held consoles and smartphones). The majority of television screens and monitors have liquid crystal displays (LCDs). The best LCD screens have light-emitting diode (LED) backlighting, and are often called LED displays.

Force and touch feedback

Feel the thud as your wrestling opponent whacks you or the pressure on your wheels as you screech a round a corner! That's the job of force feedback. The most common force-feedback system is vibration

(or "rumble"), created by spinning off-center weights inside hand-held game controllers. Top-end steering wheels and flight sticks feature motors that provide force feedback as they are turned or twisted.

Touch feedback is technically known as haptics. Future consoles may provide feedback for haptic gloves, which allow players to feel objects in game worlds, even though the objects don't physically exist!

A haptic glove allows touch feedback. Controlled by the computer, it presses on a player's fingers, giving the impression that the player is touching an object.

Three-dimensional displays Three-dimensions (3D) is the great new technology at the movies, with films such as *Avatar* wowing audiences. This amazing technology is coming to the world of computer games.

In the real world, our eyes let us see in 3D. They give us a sense of depth so we can tell how far away objects are. The trick of 3D technology is to make the flat (2D) images on a screen look 3D. These displays fool your eyes into seeing 3D images by displaying two images at once—one for the left eye and one for the right eye. The difficulty is making sure only the correct eye sees the correct image.

The simplest way of achieving 3D is known as anaglyph. The computer creates one image normally in red and another normally in blue, and overlays one on the other. When viewed through

This is a type of 3D image known as an anaglyph, which appears in 3D when viewed through tinted glasses.

glasses with red and blue filters, the image appears in 3D. A superior system is based on shutter glasses. Images for the right eye and then for the left eye are

HOW IT WORKS

The shutter-glasses approach to 3D means a screen must be able to display twice as many images per second as normal. For smooth animation, a 120 Hertz screen is required. Only some TV and computer monitor companies are making these, and they are more expensive than standard screens. On personal computers, special graphics cards are needed to run these screens.

displayed on screen in quick succession. The glasses make sure only the correct image reaches each eye.

Games that make use of 3D technology are just being released. A game based on the movie *Avatar* is the first to make use of shutter-glass technology.

Producing 3D images requires plenty of graphics processing power because every frame must be rendered twice as there are two slightly different viewpoints.

NVIDIA's GeForce 3D Vision system uses a custom screen and glasses to create the 3D effect.

WHAT'S NEXT?

A different approach to 3D is to use a system called head tracking. The player wears a transmitter on his or her head and a sensor linked to the game platform detects its position. An alternative is a webcam with software that tracks head movement. When the player moves left or right, the computer adjusts the picture on screen, giving the impression of 3D.

Virtual reality You've probably heard the phrase "virtual reality" many times, but what exactly is it? And how will it affect computer games? The idea is to combine many technologies—screens, sound, motion feedback—to make your gaming experience so realistic you'll be convinced you're in the game world. It's the ultimate gaming technology!

Virtual reality starts with 3D graphics on a 3D display. In addition, the display must fill the player's field of vision, shutting out the real world.

This can be achieved with a huge screen, smaller screens side by side, or a virtual reality headset. The display system must also track the player's

IMMERSION

In the world of games, the term "immersion" refers to how you become absorbed in a game while you play. You forget where you really are and feel as though you are in the world of the game. Immersion is achieved by a combination of technologies. To start with, a game must have interesting game play. Then come realistic graphics and sound. The closer to a living, breathing world the game can get, the more immersive the game will be. Gesture control aids immersion because it provides a realistic way of interacting with the game world and its characters.

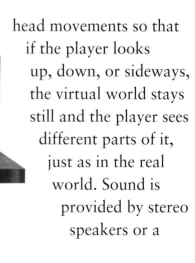

head movements so that if the player looks up, down, or sideways, the virtual world stays still and the player sees different parts of it, just as in the real world. Sound is provided by stereo speakers or a

Screens that fill a player's field of vision (this is a multi-screen system called Eyefinity from AMD (Advanced Micro Devices)) help to immerse the player in a game.

A virtual reality headset—in this case the iWear VR920—displays 3D images on tiny screens inside the set and produces stereo sound from its earphones.

surround sound system. Force feedback and haptics are required (see page 37) so the player can touch, move, and feel objects in the world. Motion sensors and gesture control are also required.

All these technologies are available now, but virtual reality systems are not yet popular due to expense and lack of games developed for them.

HOW IT WORKS

Inside a virtual-reality headset are two small, high-definition screens, one for each of the player's eyes. These display two slightly different images of the game world to produce a 3D image. Lenses allow the player's eyes to focus on the screens. The headset also includes stereo headphones.

conclusion

Computer game web sites and magazines are full of news about cutting-edge games, new consoles, and other gaming technology. There is a constant stream of new ideas. But where is gaming technology really heading?

It's very difficult to predict a year ahead in the gaming industry, let alone five or ten years ahead, as console developers keep their new ideas secret for as long as possible. However, there are some obvious trends.

For a start, electronics will become faster and more powerful, allowing more complex games, better graphics, and a more realistic gaming experience.

With more poweful electronics come a march toward living, breathing worlds, photorealism, and complete immersion in games.

Convergence is another trend. For example, instead of game consoles that only play games, we now have consoles that are media hubs and communication

Gaming technology has many applications. In South Korea, golfers can visit virtual golf centers. Sensors detect the flight of the ball and a computer generates images of the course.

MORE THAN GAMES

The technologies designed mainly for computer games are important for training and teaching, too. They are used in computer simulations for training by pilots, student drivers, and sailors, allowing people to learn in a safe environment. Even firefighters are using gaming technology to practice in simulated dangerous environments.

devices, and mobile phones that are also cameras and game machines. In the future, we might have televisions that are also gaming machines.

Social issues of game technology

How many hours a day do you play computer games? Do others think it's too many? It's always tempting to have one more shot at a game level, isn't it? Some people (children and adults) become addicted to playing games, spending hours every day at their consoles. They don't get any exercise, don't interact with other people, and even lie about their addiction.

But it's not all bad news. There is evidence that playing games helps hand-eye coordination and problem-solving skills, and some games even encourage fitness. Multi-player games also encourage team building and cooperation. Some games can be used for education and training.

As gaming technology progresses, it is harder to imagine a world without some kind of video games. Even if we don't know what gaming will be like in the future, we know that it will be around and constantly evolving.

A player obviously engrossed in a console game. But has he been playing for too many hours? Is he becoming addicted to the game?

WHAT'S NEXT?

So, what's gaming going to be like in the distant future? Still on consoles and TVs? Or perhaps on huge 3D screens attached to online gaming servers with gesture control. Or it might be in a completely new way that nobody has yet thought of, using some new way of interacting with game worlds and characters. Perhaps by 2050 we will spend more time playing in virtual worlds than living in the real one!

glossary

artificial intelligence the science of making computers behave in a way that people would

Blu-ray disc an optical disc that holds up to four times as much data as a DVD, named because it is read by a blue-colored laser

capacitor an electronic component that stores electricity

console an electronic machine designed solely for playing video games

core the part of a computer's processing unit (either a central processing unit or a graphics processing unit) that actually does the processing

first-person game a video game in which the player controls a character in a game world, seeing the action from the character's point of view

game engine the software that controls the progress of a game

game controller a device that allows a player to control games using buttons, sticks, wheels, and so on

graphics card a plug-in card for a personal computer that contains a graphics processor and other hardware for drawing graphics and playing video

hard drive a computer storage device that records data on a hard magnetic disc

hardware the physical parts of a computer, such as the microchips, graphics card, disc drives, and so on

hydraulics using liquids inside pumps, pipes, cylinders, and pistons to transfer force and movement from one place to another

infrared invisible red rays given off by a warm object

language code for a computer, written using a particular set of instructions

light-emitting diode an electronic device that emits light when electricity passes through it by blocking the flow of electricity in one direction

megabit a million bits of information

nanotechnology creating machines on an incredibly tiny scale by using atoms and molecules as building blocks

optical drive a computer disc drive that reads information from and writes information to an optical disc such as a CD or DVD

pixel short for picture element, one of the dots that make up an image produced by a computer

pneumatics using air inside pumps, pipes, cylinders, and pistons to transfer force and movement from one place to another

rendering creating a computer image of a game world from the data that describes the world

resistor an electronic component that restricts the flow of electricity

silicon the substance that many electronic components, including transistors and microchips, are made from

software instructions that tell a computer how to work and what job to do, and the data that it processes

sound card a plug-in card for a personal computer that creates hi-fi sound and sound effects

transistor an electronic component that works like a switch, turning the flow of electricity on or off

webcam a small video camera attached to a personal computer that takes video to be sent over the internet

wi-fi a wireless networking system that allows computers to connect to a network using radio waves

more information

Books

Gamers Unite!: The Video Game Revolution by Shane Frederick, Compass Point Books, 2010.

Video Games by Chris Jozefowicz, Gareth Stevens Pub, 2010.

Web sites

Showcasing rare video games and video game history *http://www.videogamemuseum.com*

How 3D images are created by computer *http://computer.howstuffworks.com/ 3dgraphics.htm*

All about NVIDIA's graphics processors, including the 3D system *http://www.nvidia.com*

All about AMD's graphics processors *http://www.amd.com*

Places to visit

Computer History Museum
Mountain View, California
Visit one of the world's largest collections of computing artifacts.
http://www.computerhistory.org

The American Classic Arcade Museum at Funspot
Laconia, New Hampshire
An arcade full of classic video games.
http://www.classicarcademuseum.org

Museum of Science
Boston, Massachusetts
Includes exhibits and presentations on computer technology.
http://www.mos.org

index

Numbers in *italic* refer to illustrations.